DISCARD

PLAY WITH Paper

by Sara Lynn and Diane James

Carolrhoda Books, Inc. / Minneapolis

Play with Paper

Here are some ideas for using paper in different ways. Use these suggestions for making collages, cards, decorations, and lots more!

Crumpled Paper

Crumple a piece of paper in your hands, then flatten it out again. Look at the pattern you've made. Try making a collage out of crumpled paper.

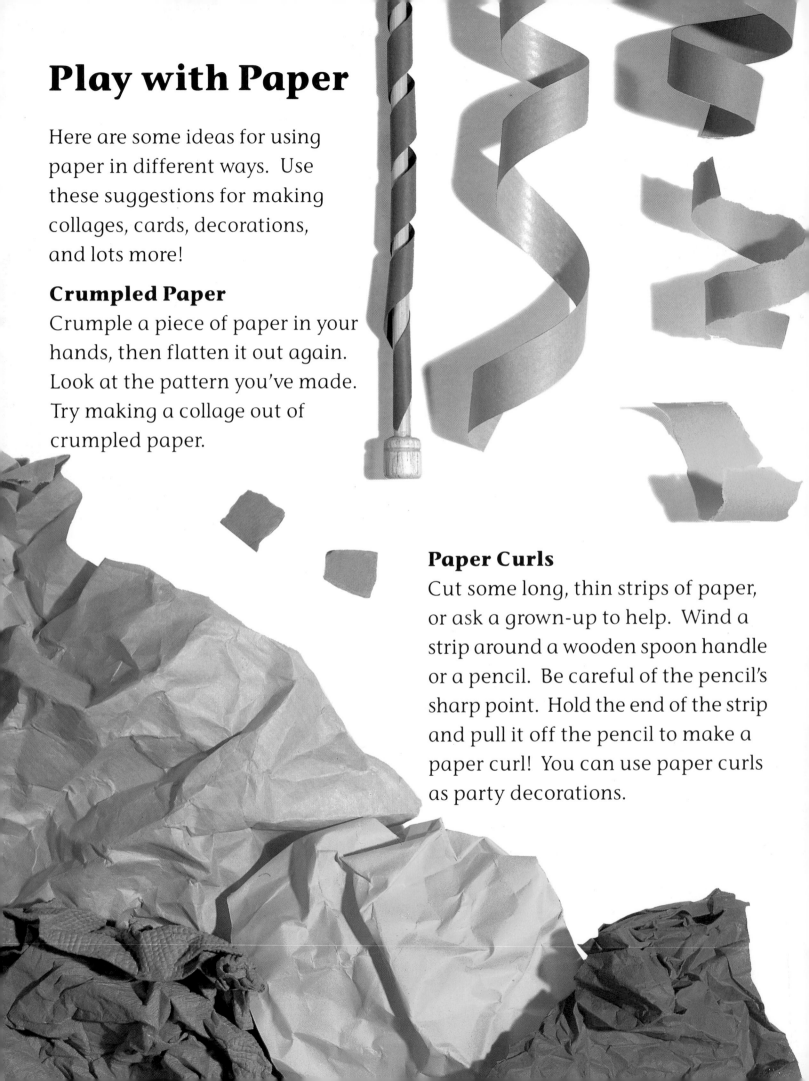

Paper Curls

Cut some long, thin strips of paper, or ask a grown-up to help. Wind a strip around a wooden spoon handle or a pencil. Be careful of the pencil's sharp point. Hold the end of the strip and pull it off the pencil to make a paper curl! You can use paper curls as party decorations.

Torn Paper

When you cut paper with scissors, its edges are straight. But if you tear paper into shapes, the edges will be rough. Make a collection of many different shapes of torn paper. Sort them into separate piles by color and shape. Then use them to make a picture.

Fun Fish

It's easy to make colorful fish like these. Look at the fish on the next few pages to get ideas for making and decorating your fish.

Try using different types of paper to make your fish—old wrapping paper, newspaper, paper napkins, and construction paper.

Ask a grown-up to help you cut
some fish shapes like these from
thin cardboard.

Cut out pieces of colored paper
slightly larger than your fish shapes.
Glue a piece of paper to one of the
fish. Carefully tear the paper around
the edge of the cardboard.

Now it's time to decorate your fish! Look at pictures of real fish to see what beautiful colors they are. Try using some of the ideas here, or make up some new ones of your own.

You can decorate a fish with paper curls, as we did on page 5. Tear small triangles from colored paper and curl them around a pencil. This green fish is decorated with pieces of torn paper.

Tear squares from colored paper to make a polka-dot fish. Fold long strips of colored paper back and forth like an accordion to make a striped fish.

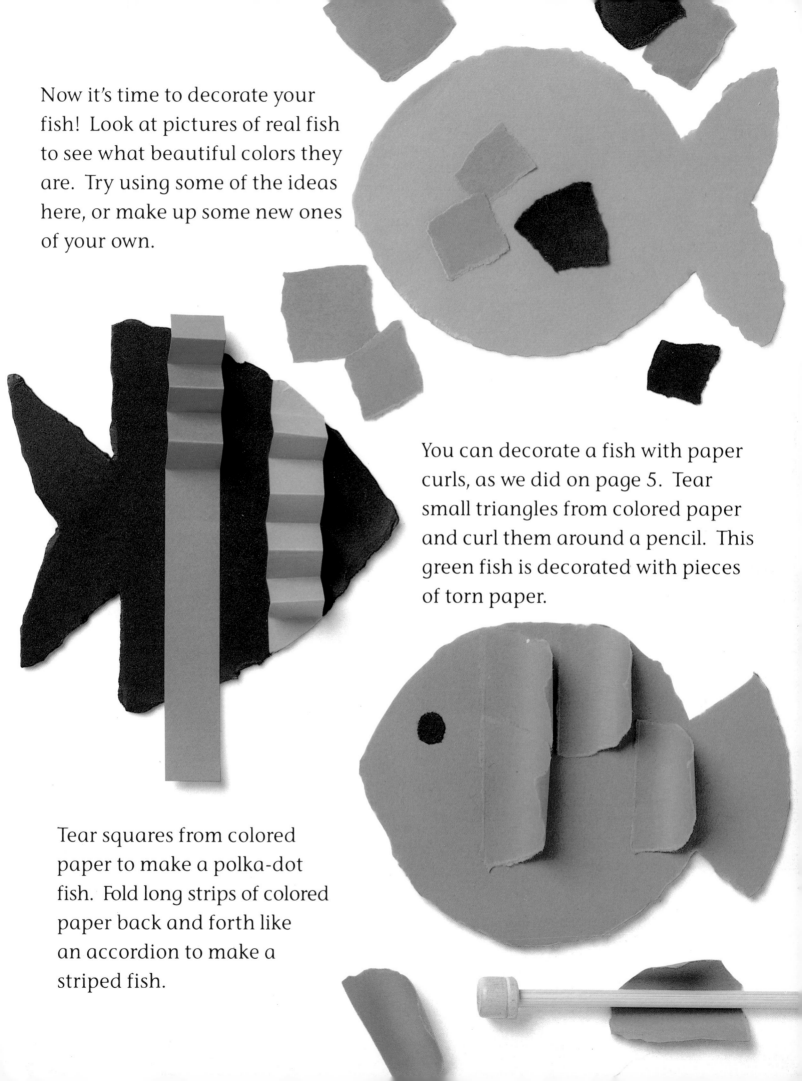

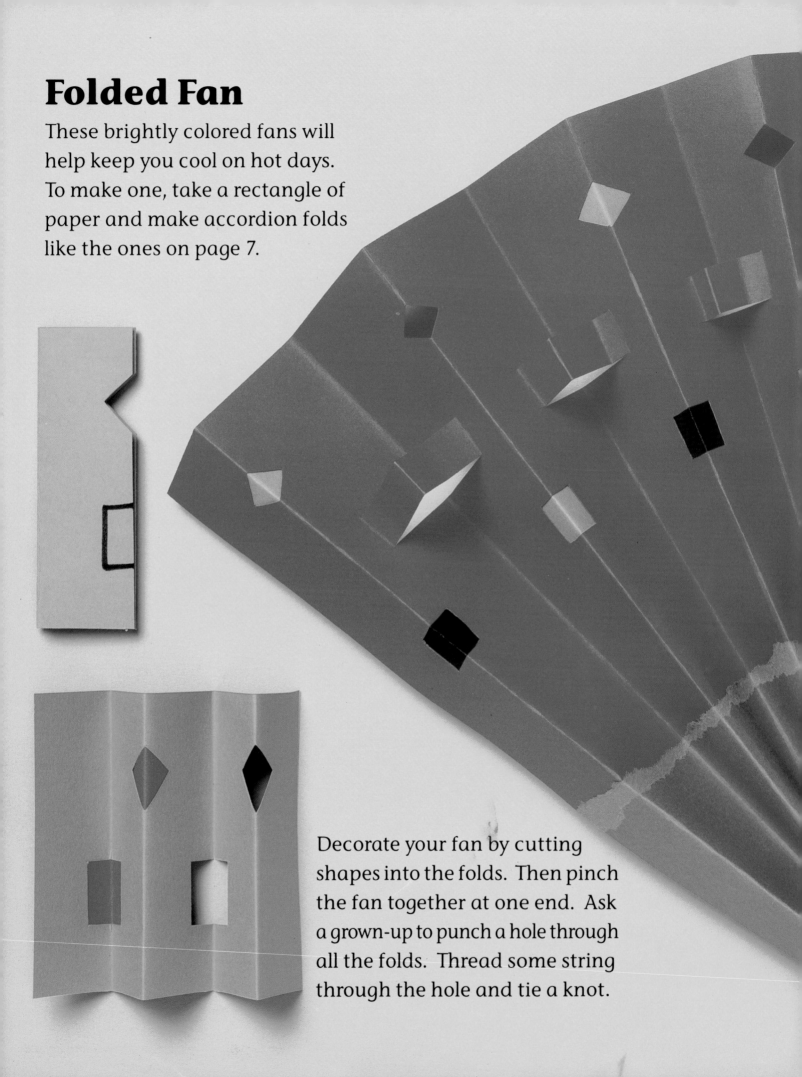

Folded Fan

These brightly colored fans will help keep you cool on hot days. To make one, take a rectangle of paper and make accordion folds like the ones on page 7.

Decorate your fan by cutting shapes into the folds. Then pinch the fan together at one end. Ask a grown-up to punch a hole through all the folds. Thread some string through the hole and tie a knot.

Paper Beads

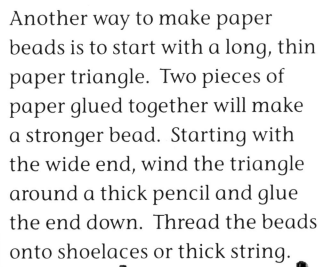

Cut some long strips of paper, or ask a grown-up to help. Roll a strip around the handle of a wooden spoon. Put a dab of glue on the end of the strip to seal your paper bead.

Another way to make paper beads is to start with a long, thin paper triangle. Two pieces of paper glued together will make a stronger bead. Starting with the wide end, wind the triangle around a thick pencil and glue the end down. Thread the beads onto shoelaces or thick string.

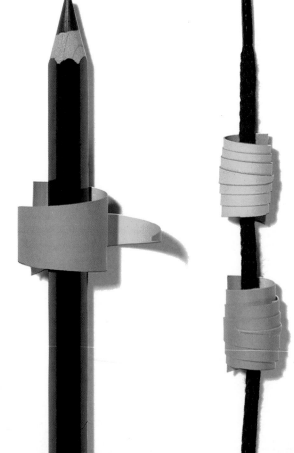

Animal Masks

Pretend to be a giant, cuddly bear! Glue some light brown paper onto a sheet of cardboard. Ask a grown-up to trace the bear's head on the next page. Tape the tracing to the cardboard and cut around it. Cut out two holes for the bear's eyes. Cut out ears and a nose from colored paper and glue them onto your mask.

Ask a grown-up to make small holes on either side of the mask and thread some elastic through the holes. Make a knot at each end of the elastic to keep it from slipping through.

What other kinds of bears can you make? How about a polar bear? Now turn the page to see some other animal masks that you can make.

The next time you have a party, ask
all your friends to come as animals!

Roar! Here's a tiger mask. What other
sorts of masks could you make? Try
making a monster mask.

Bunch of Flowers

This beautiful bunch of flowers is made from paper napkins! Take a napkin out of its package. Fold it in half to make a triangle. Make sure the folded edges are on top. Now fold the triangle again, as shown.

Cut straight across the top of the triangle and unfold the napkin. You should have a circle. Pinch the center of the circle together and twist it tight. Put a drop of glue on the end of the twisted part and poke it into the top of a straw.

Fold-and-Cut Animals

You can make an animal parade!

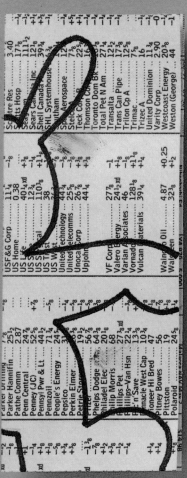

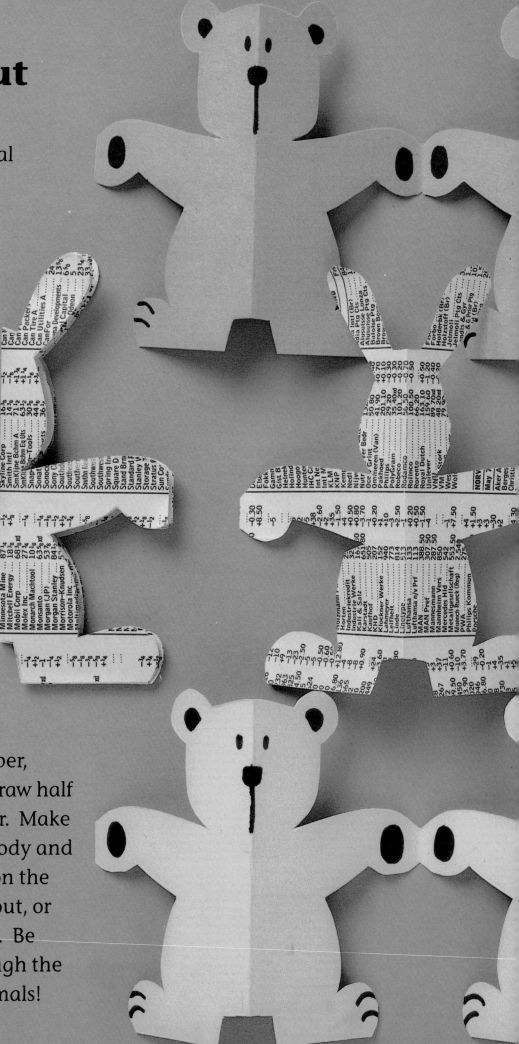

Fold a long strip of thin paper, such as newspaper, into accordion folds. Draw half an animal on the paper. Make sure the middle of its body and the end of its paw are on the folds. Cut the animal out, or ask a grown-up to help. Be careful not to cut through the folds. Unfold your animals!

Torn-Paper Pictures

Here is an easy way for you to make cards for all your friends. First, fold a rectangle of thin cardboard in half to make the background for your card. Then ask a grown-up for two jar lids, one bigger than the other.

Put one lid on a square of colored paper and carefully tear the paper around the outside to make a circle. Do the same with the other lid. Use the circles to decorate your card. You can make animals, as we did, or make your own designs.

Here is an idea for making a picture to decorate your room. Collect some colored paper—even small scraps will be useful. You'll also need glue and a piece of construction paper to make the background of your picture.

When you have decided what you want your picture to look like, start tearing paper shapes. We started with the tree and the snake. Next, we added the grass and flowers, and then the tiger.

Photo acknowledgments:
pp. 2, 3, 4, 5, 10, 11, 12, 13, 14, 15, Jon Barnes;
pp. 6, 7, 8, 9, 16, 17, 18, 19, 20, 21, 22, 23, Toby.

This edition published 1993
by Carolrhoda Books, Inc.

Lobrary of Congress Cataloging-in-Publication Data

Lynn, Sara.
  Play with paper / by Sara Lynn and Diane James.
     p.   cm.
  "First published in 1991 by Two-Can Publishing . . . London"
—CIP T.p. verso.
  Summary: Describes how to make a variety of paper crafts,
including fish, flowers, and masks.
  ISBN 0-87614-754-6
  1. Paper work—Juvenile literature. [1. Paper work. 2. Handicraft.]
I. James, Diane. II. Title.
TT870.L96   1993
745.54—dc20
                                        91-46110
                                          CIP
                                          AC

Manufactured in the United States of America

1 2 3 4 5 6 7 8 9 10 02 01 00 99 98 97 96 95 94 93

DEMCO